The Ultimate Pennsylvania Guide for Kids

Julia Wolff

Foreword

Welcome to *The Ultimate Pennsylvania Guide for Kids*—a journey through one of America's most fascinating, fun-filled, and history-rich states. Whether you've lived in Pennsylvania your whole life or you're just discovering it for the first time, this book is your all-in-one passport to explore everything that makes the Keystone State so special.

From the rolling hills of the Poconos to the towering skylines of Philadelphia and Pittsburgh, Pennsylvania is full of surprises. It's a place where chocolate flows from a town named Hershey, where a groundhog predicts the weather, and where you can ride roller coasters, tour underground coal mines, and hike to stunning waterfalls—all in one weekend.

But Pennsylvania is more than just exciting attractions. It's the birthplace of American independence, home to amazing inventors and athletes, and a state that changes with the seasons in the most magical ways. It's filled with people from many backgrounds and cultures, and it offers something for every kind of kid—whether you're into sports, science, art, history, or simply adventure.

This book was written just for you: curious, creative, and ready to learn. Inside, you'll find facts, stories, games, and surprises that bring Pennsylvania to life. You'll learn not just where places are, but why they matter—and why this state has played such an important role in shaping the country.

So open your eyes wide, grab a pencil for some fun activities, and get ready to explore the people, places, food, nature, and wild, wonderful facts of Pennsylvania. Let's hit the road—and discover what makes this state truly unforgettable.

Chapter 1: Welcome to Pennsylvania!

When you hear the name *Pennsylvania*, what do you picture? Maybe the Liberty Bell or a Philly cheesesteak? How about green rolling hills, horse-drawn buggies, or even a world-famous groundhog named Punxsutawney Phil? Whether you're a total beginner or already know a few fun facts, you're about to discover why Pennsylvania is one of the coolest, most fascinating states in the entire country.

Let's start our journey by learning where Pennsylvania is and why it's so important in American history.

Where is Pennsylvania on the Map?

Pennsylvania is part of the **Northeastern United States**, tucked between the Atlantic Coast and the Midwest. It's not a coastal state, but it still plays a big role in connecting different parts of the country. You could think of it as the bridge between New York City's skyscrapers and Ohio's open farmland.

It borders **six different states**:

- **New York** to the north

- **New Jersey** to the east

- **Delaware** and **Maryland** to the south

- **West Virginia** to the southwest

- **Ohio** to the west

That means you could drive in almost any direction and end up in another state in just a few hours!

Even though it doesn't sit directly on the Atlantic Ocean, Pennsylvania **does touch water in important ways**. In the northwest corner of the state, it reaches **Lake Erie**, one of the five Great Lakes. This gives the state access to important shipping routes. And through the **Delaware River**, boats can travel to and from the Atlantic Ocean. Pennsylvania may not have sandy beaches, but it still has serious water power!

Why is it Called the Keystone State?

You've probably heard Pennsylvania's nickname: **The Keystone State**. But what's a keystone?

In architecture, a **keystone** is the center stone in a stone arch. Without it, the whole arch would collapse. It's the piece that holds everything together. During the time when the United States was forming, Pennsylvania was right in the middle—**geographically, politically, and socially**.

Here's how:

- It was one of the original **13 colonies**.

- **Philadelphia** was the site of the signing of both the **Declaration of Independence** and the **U.S. Constitution**.

- Pennsylvania was an early leader in industry and transportation, helping to "hold up" the country's economy.

So, just like a keystone in an arch, Pennsylvania held the young nation together. That's a pretty big job!

Some Basic Facts to Know

Now that you know where it is and why it matters, let's check out a few **quick facts** about the state:

- **Capital City**: Harrisburg

- **Biggest City**: Philadelphia

- **Population**: About 13 million people

- **Land Area**: Over 46,000 square miles—big enough to fit all of New Jersey and still have room!

- **Statehood**: Became the 2nd state in the U.S. on December 12, 1787

Pennsylvania also has a **state flag** featuring the state coat of arms: two horses, a ship, a plow, and three sheaves of wheat. It's all about hard work, trade, and agriculture—things Pennsylvania has always been known for.

You'll also find state symbols that represent the natural beauty of PA:

- **State Bird**: Ruffed Grouse – a plump little bird that drums its wings in the forest

- **State Flower**: Mountain Laurel – known for its beautiful pink and white blossoms

- **State Tree**: Eastern Hemlock – a sturdy evergreen tree found all over PA's forests

---

First Impressions: What Makes Pennsylvania Cool?

So what do kids usually think is **awesome** about Pennsylvania?

- **It's full of firsts!** First zoo (Philadelphia Zoo), first computer, first baseball stadium, and even the first American flag legend!

- **Chocolate lovers rejoice.** It's the home of **Hershey**, known as the Sweetest Place on Earth.

- **History is everywhere.** From the Liberty Bell to Civil War battlefields, you'll be stepping into the past at every turn.

- **It has amazing amusement parks.** Ever heard of Hersheypark or Knoebels? PA has rides, roller coasters, and water fun for all ages.

- **Nature fans are in for a treat.** There are waterfalls, mountains, lakes, and more trails than you could hike in a year.

- **You'll see buggies next to cars.** In places like Lancaster, the **Amish people** live a simple, old-fashioned lifestyle that's really interesting to learn about.

What's Coming Up?

In this guide, we'll dive into **battles and bridges, cities and small towns, famous Pennsylvanians**, and even **weird local traditions** (like how one groundhog predicts the weather each year). You'll learn how Pennsylvania helped shape the United States—and discover just how much fun this state has to offer.

Ready to explore? Let's go!

Chapter 2: From Past to Present — The History of Pennsylvania

Pennsylvania has one of the richest and most exciting histories of any state in America. From the peaceful tribes who first called the land home, to the bold thinkers who helped form a new nation, and on to the steel and coal industries that powered America's future—Pennsylvania has always been a place where big things happen.

Let's take a journey through time to see how Pennsylvania went from forests and rivers to factories and railroads—and became one of the most important states in the country.

Before Europeans: Native Tribes

Long before William Penn or George Washington ever set foot here, Pennsylvania was home to powerful and wise Native American tribes. Among the most well-known were the **Lenape**, the **Susquehannock**, and the **Erie people**.

- The **Lenape** (also called the Delaware people) lived in the eastern part of Pennsylvania. They were skilled hunters, fishermen, and farmers who grew corn, beans, and squash—known as the "Three Sisters."

- The **Susquehannock** lived along the Susquehanna River and built large, fortified villages. They were fierce warriors and excellent traders.

- The **Erie people** lived in the northwest and got their name from the Great Lake nearby. They were also

13

known for their bark-covered longhouses and canoes.

These tribes formed **networks of trade, shared resources,** and respected nature. They lived in harmony with the land, moving with the seasons and using every part of the animals they hunted. Long before roads or railways, the rivers of Pennsylvania served as natural highways for travel and trade.

William Penn and the Quakers

Fast forward to the 1600s, when European settlers began arriving. Among them was a man who would change Pennsylvania forever—**William Penn.**

William Penn was an Englishman and a **Quaker**—a member of a Christian group that believed in peace, fairness, and equality. At the time, Quakers were treated unfairly in England, so Penn wanted to create a place where people could **worship freely** and **live without fear.**

In 1681, the King of England gave Penn a large piece of land in the New World to settle a debt. That land would become **Pennsylvania**, which means "Penn's Woods."

Penn called it his **"Holy Experiment"**—a colony where people of all religions could live in peace. He treated Native Americans with unusual respect for the time, signing **peace treaties** and paying for the land rather than taking it by force.

Penn's city of **Philadelphia**, which means "City of Brotherly Love," became a place where people from many countries and religions could start fresh. It would soon grow to be one of the most important cities in the colonies.

Colonial Life and Growth

As more settlers arrived, Pennsylvania began to grow quickly. Colonists built **farms, towns, and schools**, and trade with Native tribes continued—although not always peacefully.

- The city of **Philadelphia** became the largest city in the colonies for a time.

- The colony was known for its **diverse population**, including Germans, Scots-Irish, Dutch, and others.

- **Grain farming** made Pennsylvania the "breadbasket" of the colonies, and exports flowed out through its busy ports.

At first, many colonists and Native Americans lived side by side. But as more land was taken, conflicts began. Though William Penn had tried to keep things fair, not everyone followed his example. Over time, many Native tribes were pushed out or suffered greatly as colonists spread westward.

Revolutionary and Civil War Times

When it came time for the American colonies to **break free from British rule**, Pennsylvania was front and center. Some of the biggest moments in U.S. history happened right here.

- In **1776**, the **Declaration of Independence** was signed in **Independence Hall** in Philadelphia.

- The **Continental Congress** met in Pennsylvania to plan the revolution.

- The state was a key battlefield during the war for independence.

Decades later, during the **Civil War**, Pennsylvania again became a turning point in history. The most famous event? The **Battle of Gettysburg** in 1863.

- Gettysburg was the **bloodiest battle** of the war and marked a turning point in favor of the Union.

- President **Abraham Lincoln** delivered the **Gettysburg Address** there, reminding the country of its core values of freedom and unity.

- Pennsylvania supplied thousands of troops and resources to the Union army.

Both wars showed that Pennsylvania was not just part of history—it was shaping it.

Modern Milestones

After the wars, Pennsylvania moved into the age of industry and invention. By the 1800s and early 1900s, the state became a **powerhouse of steel, coal, railroads, and oil**.

- **Pittsburgh** became known as the **Steel City**, home to massive factories that helped build bridges, skyscrapers, and ships.

- **Scranton** and other cities grew around **coal mining,** which powered trains and homes across the country.

- The **first oil well in the U.S.** was drilled in **Titusville, Pennsylvania** in 1859.

- Pennsylvania also played a big part in the rise of **railroads,** making it easier to move goods and people across the nation.

But life wasn't easy for everyone. **Labor movements** began to fight for better working conditions, fair pay, and safer factories. Children as young as 10 worked long hours in dangerous jobs. Over time, thanks to protests and new laws, workers in Pennsylvania helped improve life for millions of Americans.

From Then to Now

Today, Pennsylvania is a blend of **past and present**. You can still walk the cobblestone streets of old Philadelphia, or stand where Lincoln gave one of the most famous speeches in history. At the same time, you can visit cutting-edge science museums, explore bustling cities, and ride roller coasters in modern amusement parks.

Whether it's Native American heritage, colonial courage, or industrial innovation, **Pennsylvania's history is packed with stories**—and they all helped shape the state we know today.

And guess what? This is just the beginning. There's so much more to explore!

Chapter 3: Famous Cities and Small Town Charms

Pennsylvania is a state with big cities full of history, art, and sports—and small towns that feel like something out of a storybook. Whether you're climbing the Rocky Steps in Philadelphia or strolling through a tiny chocolate town, each place has something special to share.

Let's take a tour through Pennsylvania's most famous cities and its charming hidden gems!

Philadelphia: The Birthplace of America

If you've ever read about the American Revolution, chances are **Philadelphia** was mentioned. That's because this city is where the United States was *born*. Known as the **"Birthplace of America,"** Philadelphia was where both the **Declaration of Independence** and the **U.S. Constitution** were written and signed.

In Philly, you'll find amazing landmarks that bring history to life:

- **The Liberty Bell**: This world-famous cracked bell once rang to call people together during the fight for independence. You can see it today at Independence National Historical Park.

- **Independence Hall**: The very building where the Founding Fathers debated and signed America's most important documents.

- **Betsy Ross House**: A tiny house where legend says Betsy Ross sewed the first American flag.

But Philly isn't just for history buffs. It's also full of fun!

- Run up the **Rocky Steps** in front of the Philadelphia Museum of Art, just like the famous movie boxer.

- Try a **Philly cheesesteak**, a sandwich made with thin-sliced beef, melted cheese, and a long hoagie roll. Locals argue over who makes it best—Pat's or Geno's!

- Visit museums, science centers, and the Philadelphia Zoo (the first in the U.S.!)

Pittsburgh: The Steel City with a Modern Twist

Across the state in the west is **Pittsburgh**, once called the **"Steel City"** because of the huge steel factories that filled the city in the 1800s and 1900s. Back then, smoke filled the sky, and workers helped build America's bridges, trains, and buildings.

Today, Pittsburgh is totally transformed. The factories are mostly gone, and in their place are **parks, museums, tech companies, and art galleries**.

Some of Pittsburgh's coolest features include:

- **More bridges than Venice, Italy**—over 400 of them! That's because three rivers meet in the middle of the city.

- **Heinz Field** and **PNC Park**, where fans cheer for the **Steelers (NFL)** and **Pirates (MLB)**.

- The **Andy Warhol Museum**, dedicated to the famous pop artist who was born in Pittsburgh.

- **Inclines** (funicular railways) that take you up Mount Washington for amazing views of the city skyline.

Pittsburgh is a mix of old and new, gritty and glamorous—making it a fascinating place to explore.

Harrisburg: The State Capital

Tucked along the **Susquehanna River, Harrisburg** may not be as big or flashy as Philly or Pittsburgh, but it plays a big role: **It's the capital of Pennsylvania!**

That means Harrisburg is where the state's most important decisions are made. Inside the **Pennsylvania State Capitol building**, lawmakers write and vote on the laws that affect everyone who lives in the state.

- The Capitol dome is topped with a **statue called "Commonwealth"**, and inside you'll find **gilded ceilings, stained glass, and murals** that make it look like a palace.

- Harrisburg also has fun places to visit like the **State Museum of Pennsylvania**, which tells the story of the state's history, nature, and inventions.

- In the spring and summer, the **Riverfront Park** is full of festivals, music, and family events.

Though it's smaller, Harrisburg plays a *huge* part in how Pennsylvania runs.

Other Notable Cities

Pennsylvania has a lot of other cities worth knowing, each with its own unique flavor.

- **Erie** sits on the edge of **Lake Erie**, one of the five Great Lakes. It's a perfect spot for swimming, boating, and even surfing in the summer! Erie is also home to **Presque Isle State Park**, a sandy beach escape with beautiful sunsets.

- **Allentown** is known for its **industrial history**, and it played an important role during the Revolutionary War when the Liberty Bell was secretly hidden there to keep it safe from the British.

- **Scranton**, once a coal mining town, became even more famous thanks to the TV show *The Office*. It's also where you can visit the **Steamtown National Historic Site**, which has real steam trains you can ride and explore.

These cities may not be as big as Philly or Pittsburgh, but they're full of surprises and local pride.

Charming Small Towns

Some of Pennsylvania's best treasures are hidden away in its **small towns**, where time moves a little slower and community feels a little stronger.

- **Jim Thorpe** is often called "The Switzerland of America" because of its beautiful **mountain setting** and European-style buildings. It's perfect for biking, hiking, or riding the old-fashioned **scenic train**.

- **Lititz** (pronounced LIT-its) is a sweet town in more ways than one. It's the home of **Wilbur Chocolate**, and it has one of the prettiest Main Streets you'll ever walk. Small shops, cozy cafes, and historic buildings make this a favorite for visitors.

- **Bedford** is known for its **charming colonial history**, old stone houses, and **natural mineral springs** that people once believed could heal illnesses.

- **Bellefonte** is full of **Victorian-era architecture**, a beautiful waterfront, and is close to **Penn State University**—which brings a fun college-town feel.

These small towns are great for weekend trips, exploring local food and shops, and experiencing the quieter side of Pennsylvania life.

A Place for Everyone

Whether you love the buzz of a busy city or the peacefulness of a country road, Pennsylvania has something just right for you. You can learn about America's past in Philadelphia, cheer for a football team in Pittsburgh, or taste chocolate in Lititz—all in the same week!

Each place in Pennsylvania tells part of the state's story. And with so many different places to visit, there's always something new to discover.

Chapter 4: The Battlefields and Freedom Trail

Pennsylvania isn't just filled with cities and nature—it's filled with **history you can walk through**. From grassy battlefields to cobblestone streets, this state holds stories that shaped America. If you've ever wondered what it would be like to stand where soldiers fought for freedom or where leaders signed the most important papers in the country's history, Pennsylvania is the place to be.

Let's explore the unforgettable sites that make Pennsylvania a living classroom of bravery, independence, and adventure.

Gettysburg: The Turning Point of the Civil War

If there's one battlefield that every American should know about, it's **Gettysburg**. This small town in southern Pennsylvania became the site of the **largest and deadliest battle** of the **Civil War**.

In **July 1863**, the Union and Confederate armies clashed for three days in and around Gettysburg. More than **50,000 soldiers were killed, wounded, or went missing**, making it the bloodiest battle ever fought on U.S. soil.

So, why does Gettysburg matter?

- It marked a major **turning point** in the Civil War, as the Union Army stopped the Confederates from invading the North.

- It inspired **President Abraham Lincoln** to give the famous **Gettysburg Address**, a short but powerful speech about democracy and honoring those who died for it.

Today, you can visit the **Gettysburg National Military Park** and:

- Walk or drive through the **battlefield**, where signs and monuments explain what happened at each location.

- Visit the **Gettysburg National Cemetery**, where Lincoln gave his speech and many soldiers are buried.

- Explore the **museum and visitor center**, where you can watch short films, see real artifacts, and view the amazing **cyclorama**—a 360-degree painting that makes you feel like you're right in the battle!

Gettysburg is not just about war—it's about learning from the past and honoring those who helped shape the future.

Valley Forge: The Winter That Tested America

Before Gettysburg, another place in Pennsylvania played a big role in America's fight for freedom—**Valley Forge**.

During the **Revolutionary War**, General **George Washington** led the Continental Army here in the winter of **1777–1778**. It wasn't a battle, but it was a big test of courage. The army faced:

- **Freezing temperatures**

- **No proper uniforms**

- **Little food or supplies**

- **Diseases like smallpox**

Even though times were tough, Washington and his men didn't give up. They trained hard, built log huts, and **became stronger and more united**. That winter helped turn them into a real fighting force.

At **Valley Forge National Historical Park**, you can:

- Walk through **reconstructed soldier cabins** and imagine life during the harsh winter.

- See **statues and monuments** honoring the bravery of the soldiers.

- Visit the **Washington's Headquarters** and learn about his leadership.

- Watch **historical reenactments**, where people dress in colonial uniforms and show how soldiers lived.

There's even a **visitor center** with exhibits and films that make history come alive. It's a great place for kids to ask questions, see real items from the war, and feel like they've stepped back in time.

Philadelphia: Where Freedom Was Signed

Before any battles were fought, the real spark of American independence started in **Philadelphia**. This city is where the country's **founding documents** were debated, written, and signed.

In **Independence Hall**, some of the greatest minds in history—like **Thomas Jefferson, Benjamin Franklin, and John Adams**—gathered to create a new nation. Here's what happened:

- In **1776**, the **Declaration of Independence** was signed, breaking away from British rule and stating that all people are created equal.

- In **1787**, the **U.S. Constitution** was written, forming the rules that still guide our country today.

Right across the street is another must-see: the **Liberty Bell**. This giant bell rang out in 1776 to call citizens to hear the first public reading of the Declaration of Independence. Today, its **famous crack** and message of liberty make it one of the most recognized symbols of freedom in the world.

Visiting these places isn't like reading about history—it's **standing where it happened.**

Historic Walking Tours and Sites

Pennsylvania makes it easy and fun to explore the past. In cities like Philadelphia, Gettysburg, and Valley Forge, you can take **walking tours** or follow **history trails** to discover even more.

Many of these tours are **kid-friendly** and feature:

- **Costumed guides** who speak like people from the 1700s.

- **Storytelling** stops where you can hear cool facts and surprising tales.

- **Hands-on museums**, where you can try on colonial clothes, play with old-fashioned tools, or even learn how to write with a quill.

Some great places to visit include:

- **The Museum of the American Revolution** in Philadelphia—full of exciting exhibits, including George Washington's real tent!

- **Franklin Court**, where you can see where Benjamin Franklin lived and printed newspapers.

- **Historic Germantown**, one of the oldest neighborhoods in America, filled with colonial houses and battle stories.

Even smaller towns often have **local museums** and **historical societies** with interesting displays and guides eager to share their town's role in Pennsylvania's story.

Time Travel in Your Own Backyard

History doesn't have to be boring. In Pennsylvania, it's **interactive, exciting, and everywhere you look**. Whether you're imagining a soldier's frozen toes at Valley Forge, ringing liberty across the world from Philadelphia, or watching cannons fire in a reenactment at Gettysburg, you'll feel like part of something big.

These battlefields and landmarks are more than places—they're reminders of how brave people came together to fight for freedom, fairness, and a future. And best of all, you can go explore them today!

Chapter 5: The Great Outdoors – Nature and Parks

If you love climbing mountains, splashing in rivers, hiking through forests, or spotting wildlife, then you're going to love Pennsylvania. The state is packed with beautiful natural places just waiting to be explored. From sparkling waterfalls to sandy beaches, from quiet birdwatching to thrilling whitewater rafting, Pennsylvania's outdoors offers something for every kind of adventurer.

Let's head outside and see what makes nature in Pennsylvania so exciting!

Mountains, Rivers, and Forests

Pennsylvania is a land of **rolling hills, winding rivers, and thick forests** that stretch as far as the eye can see. It's the kind of place where you can hike up a mountain in the morning and splash in a river by the afternoon.

- The **Appalachian Mountains** run right through the middle of the state. These ancient peaks aren't the tallest in the world, but they are full of **scenic trails**, **deep forests**, and **quiet beauty**. The **Appalachian Trail**, one of the longest hiking trails in the world, crosses through Pennsylvania—offering over **200 miles of trail** just in this state!

- The **Pocono Mountains**, located in northeastern Pennsylvania, are famous for their **outdoor fun**. People go there to ski in the winter, swim in lakes during summer, and watch the leaves change in fall. The

31

Poconos are also a great place for **fishing, tubing, and camping**.

- Two of the most important rivers in Pennsylvania are the **Delaware River** and the **Susquehanna River**. The **Delaware** forms the eastern border of the state and is perfect for **kayaking and tubing**. The **Susquehanna**, one of the longest rivers on the East Coast, winds through towns and countryside, offering **beautiful views and picnic spots** along the way.

Pennsylvania's forests are full of **oak, maple, pine, and hemlock trees**, as well as **hidden streams, wildflowers**, and **wildlife** waiting to be discovered.

State and National Parks

Pennsylvania has **over 120 state parks** and several national parks and historic sites. These are perfect places to explore nature, learn about history, and have fun with your family or friends.

Here are three especially awesome parks to check out:

- **Presque Isle State Park** (near Erie)
  This park is actually a **giant peninsula** that stretches into **Lake Erie**, forming sandy beaches and calm lagoons. You can **swim, build sandcastles, look for sea glass, and even surf** in the Great Lakes waves! In the summer, it feels more like an ocean beach than something you'd find in Pennsylvania.

- **Ricketts Glen State Park** (northeast PA)
  Want to see a waterfall—or how about **22** of them? Ricketts Glen is famous for its **Waterfall Trail**, where you can hike past one waterfall after another, each one more breathtaking than the last. You'll also find **forests older than America itself**, with trees over **300 years old**!

- **Ohiopyle State Park** (southwest PA)
  This park is an adventurer's dream. It's famous for its **whitewater rapids** on the Youghiogheny River—perfect for **rafting, kayaking, and even waterfall sliding**! There are **bike trails, hiking paths**, and natural water slides made of smooth rock.

In every part of the state, you'll find parks with **campgrounds, picnic areas, and nature centers** that make it easy for kids and families to explore safely.

Camping, Hiking, and Outdoor Fun

One of the best ways to enjoy Pennsylvania's natural beauty is to **spend a night under the stars**. Camping in a tent, camper, or even a cozy cabin lets you really experience the great outdoors.

- Many parks have **well-marked hiking trails** for all skill levels—from short, easy walks to long, rugged treks.

- You can cook over a campfire, tell stories, roast marshmallows, and watch the sky fill with stars.

- Some parks offer **guided nature hikes, evening programs**, or **junior ranger** activities just for kids.

Whether you're pitching a tent in the forest or hiking to the top of a scenic overlook, Pennsylvania's outdoor adventures help you unplug, recharge, and feel connected to nature.

Animals and Nature Watching

Pennsylvania is home to a wide variety of animals—and some of them are truly amazing to see in the wild!

- **Bald eagles** nest along rivers and lakes. With their white heads and wide wingspans, they're one of the most exciting birds to spot.

- **Black bears** live mostly in the forests of northern and central Pennsylvania. They usually stay away from people, but spotting one from a safe distance is unforgettable.

- **White-tailed deer** are common throughout the state, especially at dawn and dusk. In the fall, you might even see bucks with full antlers!

For kids who love animals and science, **bird watching** is a great hobby to try. All you need is a pair of binoculars and a notebook. You can spot **woodpeckers, blue jays, cardinals, hawks, and owls** just by being quiet and patient in the woods or even your backyard.

And in the summertime, don't forget to chase **fireflies**! Pennsylvania's fields and forests light up with glowing bugs at dusk, making every evening feel like a fairy tale.

Adventure and Seasonal Fun

Pennsylvania's **four seasons** make the outdoors exciting all year long. Each season brings its own kind of adventure:

- **Fall**: The forests burst into **reds, oranges, and golds** as the leaves change. It's the perfect time for hayrides, hikes, and cozy campfires.

- **Winter**: Snow covers the mountains, turning the Poconos and other areas into **ski and sledding hotspots**. You can try **snow tubing, ice skating, and even winter hikes**.

- **Spring**: Wildflowers bloom, birds return from migration, and the forests come alive again. It's a great time to go **creek walking** or look for **frogs and salamanders**.

- **Summer**: Warm weather means **swimming in lakes, paddling rivers, camping trips**, and **firefly-filled nights**.

No matter what time of year it is, Pennsylvania's outdoors offers new things to see and do.

Whether you're hiking up a mountain, spotting an eagle in the sky, rafting down rapids, or just roasting marshmallows under a full moon, the great outdoors of Pennsylvania is full of unforgettable experiences. There's no better way to feel connected to the natural world—and no better state to do it in!

Chapter 6: Weird, Wild, and Wacky Pennsylvania Facts

Every state has its quirks—but Pennsylvania might just win the prize for being one of the strangest, silliest, and most surprising. In between the historic landmarks and scenic parks, there are places that will make you say, "Wait, what?" From strange laws to bizarre buildings and unforgettable festivals, Pennsylvania knows how to keep things interesting.

So buckle up and get ready for a wild ride through the weirdest corners of the Keystone State!

Strange Laws

Believe it or not, there are still some **very unusual laws** on the books in Pennsylvania. Some of these rules were made a long time ago and no one ever bothered to erase them. Others were written with good intentions but sound pretty silly today.

Check these out:

- In **Scranton**, it's illegal to **sing in the bathtub**. So if you're planning a bubble bath karaoke concert... maybe just hum quietly!

- In **Morrisville**, women must have a **permit to wear makeup**. This one is never enforced—but it's still written down somewhere.

- You can't **catch fish with your hands** in Pennsylvania. That means no pretending to be a bear at the creek!

- It's also illegal to **sweep dirt under a rug** in some parts of the state. Clean honestly, folks!

- In Pittsburgh, you're technically not allowed to bring a **mule onto a trolley car**. Makes you wonder what inspired that rule…

While no one's likely to get in trouble for breaking these strange laws today, they're a fun look into how life (and lawmaking) used to be much different.

Roadside Oddities

One of the best things about road trips in Pennsylvania is spotting the **weird and wonderful roadside attractions** along the way. These eye-catching structures and sculptures are impossible to miss—and totally unforgettable.

- **The Shoe House** (in York)
  It's exactly what it sounds like: a **giant house shaped like a shoe**! Built in the 1940s by a shoe salesman, it has bedrooms, a kitchen, and even a bathroom inside the heel. Visitors can tour the house and learn its quirky history.

- **The Coffee Pot Building** (in Bedford)
  Need a morning pick-me-up? Check out this **huge coffee pot-shaped building** that once served as a lunch stand. It's now a photo stop along the Lincoln Highway.

- **Mr. Peanut Statue** (in Wilkes-Barre)
  Pennsylvania is the birthplace of Planters peanuts, and in honor of their mascot, a **giant statue of Mr. Peanut**—top hat and all—greets visitors downtown.

You'll also find giant forks, big bananas, and even a dinosaur-shaped gas station if you drive far enough. These oddities are part of what makes exploring Pennsylvania so much fun—you never know what's around the bend.

Unique Festivals

Pennsylvania knows how to throw a party—and some of those parties are as **wacky and unique** as the state itself.

- **Groundhog Day** (Punxsutawney)
  Every year on **February 2nd**, all eyes turn to a small town in western PA where a **groundhog named Punxsutawney Phil** predicts the weather. If he sees his shadow, it's six more weeks of winter. If not, spring is around the corner. Thousands of people gather at sunrise to see what the furry weather forecaster will do. It's silly, fun, and one of the most famous traditions in the country!

- **The Mushroom Festival** (Kennett Square)
  Did you know that Kennett Square is the **Mushroom Capital of the World**? Every September, this town celebrates with a two-day festival full of **mushroom-themed food, games, and contests**. There are even mushroom cook-offs and a giant

parade.

- **Firefly Festival** (Tionesta)
  When summer rolls around, Pennsylvania's forests light up with glowing fireflies. Some areas celebrate with **firefly festivals**, where families gather at night to watch the magical blinking lights and learn about these amazing insects.

- Other quirky festivals include **pickle celebrations, bug fairs, cow parades**, and even **races where people roll giant pumpkins**!

If you like unusual foods, wild costumes, and traditions you won't find anywhere else, Pennsylvania's festivals are the place to be.

Unusual Towns and Places

Some of the weirdest and most interesting things about Pennsylvania are the **towns themselves**—with strange names, spooky stories, or completely out-of-this-world features.

- **Centralia**: Once a busy coal-mining town, Centralia is now almost completely empty. Why? Because in 1962, a fire started in an underground coal mine—and it's **still burning today**, over 60 years later! The fire made the town unsafe, and most people moved away. Today, you can walk through abandoned streets with smoke rising from the ground—a **real-life ghost town**.

- **Intercourse**: Yep, it's a real town name, and it's in the heart of Amish Country. While the name might make people giggle, it comes from an old word meaning "friendship" and "fellowship." Nearby towns like **Bird-in-Hand** and **Blue Ball** also have funny names, making the area a favorite for road sign selfies.

- **Zelienople**, **Slippery Rock**, and **Noodle Doosie** (yes, that's a real place!) are other oddly named spots scattered throughout the state.

Pennsylvania's geography is filled with stories—some funny, some spooky, and all unforgettable.

The Fun Side of Pennsylvania

Sure, Pennsylvania is full of serious history, breathtaking parks, and famous cities. But it's also **delightfully weird**, and that's part of what makes it such an exciting place to explore.

Whether you're visiting a giant shoe, trying mushroom ice cream, or walking through a town with smoke rising from the ground, there's never a dull moment in the Keystone State.

So next time you're traveling through Pennsylvania, keep your eyes peeled—you never know when you'll stumble upon something totally wacky!

Chapter 7: Famous Pennsylvanians

Pennsylvania isn't just full of amazing places—it's also the birthplace or home of **some of the most famous people in history**. From brilliant inventors to world-changing athletes, and from powerful leaders to superstars of music and film, Pennsylvanians have left a mark on the world in every field you can imagine.

Let's meet some of the most legendary, inspiring, and talented people who've called the Keystone State home!

Founding Figures

Long before movie stars and musicians, Pennsylvania produced **leaders and legends** who helped shape the country.

- **Benjamin Franklin**
  Born in Boston but most famous for his life in **Philadelphia**, Ben Franklin was a true genius. He was an **inventor**, **writer**, **scientist**, **diplomat**, and one of America's most important **Founding Fathers**.
  Some of his most famous inventions include the **lightning rod**, **bifocal glasses**, and the **Franklin stove**. He also started the **first public library** and helped create the **U.S. postal system**.
  Franklin's face is even on the **$100 bill**—which is why it's sometimes called a "Ben."

- **Betsy Ross**
  According to legend, Betsy Ross sewed the **first American flag** right in her Philadelphia upholstery shop. While historians still debate the details, she's

remembered as a patriotic figure and a symbol of the important role women played during the birth of the nation.

These two aren't the only important early Pennsylvanians—but they're among the most iconic.

Musicians and Actors

Pennsylvania has produced **some of the biggest names in entertainment**, from chart-topping singers to Hollywood stars.

- **Taylor Swift**
  One of the most famous singers in the world today, Taylor Swift was born in **Reading, Pennsylvania**, and raised in nearby **Wyomissing**. She started writing songs at a young age and became a **country music star** before switching to **pop superstardom**. Her songwriting has earned her dozens of awards and millions of fans around the globe.

- **Will Smith**
  Born and raised in **Philadelphia**, Will Smith started his career as a **rapper** before starring in the hit TV show **The Fresh Prince of Bel-Air**. He later became a blockbuster movie actor in films like *Men in Black*, *Independence Day*, and *Aladdin*. Known for his charm and talent, he's one of the most successful actors of all time.

- **Tina Fey**
  A comedian, actress, and writer, Tina Fey grew up near

Upper Darby, Pennsylvania. She became famous on **Saturday Night Live** and went on to create and star in the hit comedy **30 Rock**. She also wrote the movie **Mean Girls**, which became a pop culture favorite.

Whether on stage, screen, or in music videos, these stars shine bright—and all of them started in Pennsylvania.

Athletes and Sports Heroes

Pennsylvania is home to sports fans who are passionate, loyal, and loud—and it's also home to **athletes who became legends**.

- **Kobe Bryant**
  Born in **Philadelphia**, Kobe was one of the greatest basketball players of all time. He joined the **NBA** straight out of high school and spent his entire career with the **Los Angeles Lakers**, winning **five championships**. Known for his "Mamba Mentality," Kobe inspired millions with his work ethic, talent, and passion.

- **Joe Montana**
  Raised in **Monongahela**, Montana became a legendary **NFL quarterback**. He played for the **San Francisco 49ers** and won **four Super Bowls**. He was known for staying cool under pressure and is often ranked among the greatest quarterbacks in football history.

- **Dan Marino**
  Born in **Pittsburgh**, Dan Marino became a star quarterback for the **Miami Dolphins**. He broke several passing records during his career and is known for his quick release and powerful arm. Marino was also inducted into the **Pro Football Hall of Fame**.

These athletes didn't just win games—they became **icons** who inspired kids everywhere to chase their dreams and give it their all.

Modern Innovators and Authors

Pennsylvania also has a long list of people who made the world better through **science, writing, and creativity**.

- **Rachel Carson**
  Born in **Springdale, Pennsylvania**, Rachel Carson was a **marine biologist and author** who helped launch the modern **environmental movement**. Her book **Silent Spring** warned people about harmful pesticides and inspired new laws to protect nature. Thanks to her work, people around the world began to care more about the environment.

- **Jeff Goldblum**
  A beloved actor with a unique voice and quirky charm, Jeff Goldblum was born in **West Homestead, PA**. He starred in hit movies like *Jurassic Park*, *Independence Day*, and *The Fly*. He's also a jazz musician and hosts a fun educational show called *The World According to*

Jeff Goldblum.

- **Jerry Spinelli**
  An award-winning author from **Norristown**, Jerry
  Spinelli writes books for kids and teens that are full of
  heart, humor, and real-life struggles. His most famous
  book, **Maniac Magee**, tells the story of a boy who
  becomes a legend in his town while dealing with racism
  and homelessness. He's also known for *Stargirl*, *Loser*,
  and many other beloved novels.

These modern Pennsylvanians have changed the world in
thoughtful, creative ways—through words, science, and
storytelling.

Proud to Be from Pennsylvania

From founding fathers to pop stars, from scientists to sports
legends, the list of **famous Pennsylvanians** goes on and on.
They've made the world laugh, learn, cheer, think, and dream.

One of the best parts of learning about these incredible
people? Realizing that **they all started as kids**, just like you.
They walked the same streets, played in the same parks, and
went to schools in towns across the Keystone State.

Who knows? Maybe the next great inventor, musician, or hero
is reading this book right now.

Chapter 8: Pennsylvania's Role in American Government

Pennsylvania has played a starring role in the story of the United States government. From the very beginning of America's founding to the way it runs today, the Keystone State has been a **center of ideas, decisions, and leadership**. Whether it was helping shape democracy or continuing to make important state laws today, Pennsylvania has always been a place where voices are heard and freedom is protected.

Let's take a closer look at how Pennsylvania helped build the American government—and how it still plays a big part today.

Colonial Government and Democracy

When most people think of early America, they imagine British kings, colonies, and strict rules. But Pennsylvania was **different from the start**, thanks to one man's bold ideas.

- **William Penn**, the founder of Pennsylvania, believed in **fairness, freedom, and equality**. He was a **Quaker**, and he wanted his new colony to be a place where people of different religions could live together in peace.

- He introduced some of the **first democratic principles** in the colonies. Instead of a government where only the wealthy had power, Penn allowed **citizens to vote**, **create laws**, and **choose leaders**. This was a radical idea at the time!

- In 1701, he wrote the **Pennsylvania Charter of Privileges**, which gave colonists rights like **freedom of**

religion, the right to **fair trials**, and protection from unfair taxes. This charter helped **inspire the Bill of Rights** in the U.S. Constitution many years later.

In a way, Pennsylvania was like a **testing ground for democracy**, where the values of freedom and justice got their start before spreading across the country.

Important Documents and Decisions

No state played a bigger role in **the birth of America** than Pennsylvania. It was in **Philadelphia** where leaders from all 13 colonies met to decide the future of the country.

- In **1776**, inside **Independence Hall**, brave leaders like **Thomas Jefferson, John Adams**, and **Benjamin Franklin** signed the **Declaration of Independence**. This document told Great Britain that the colonies wanted to be **free and independent**, and it explained that all people have the right to **life, liberty, and the pursuit of happiness**.

- Just a few years later, in **1787**, the same room saw the writing of the **U.S. Constitution**—the document that created the **framework of American government**. It set up the three branches of government, the checks and balances system, and the powers of each state and citizen.

These two documents—both created in Pennsylvania—are among the **most important in world history**. And you can still visit the room where it all happened today!

How the State Government Works

While the federal government (based in Washington, D.C.) makes laws for the entire country, each state—including Pennsylvania—has its **own government** too.

Pennsylvania's government has **three branches**, just like the federal one:

1. **Executive Branch** – This includes the **Governor**, who is like the president of the state. The governor **signs laws, manages emergencies**, and **leads state departments**.

2. **Legislative Branch** – This is made up of two groups: the **Pennsylvania House of Representatives** and the **Pennsylvania Senate**. These elected leaders **create laws, approve budgets**, and **represent the people**.

3. **Judicial Branch** – These are the **courts and judges**, who make sure laws are followed and decide what's fair and legal.

Pennsylvania's **Capitol Building in Harrisburg** is where these leaders work. You can even take a tour and watch government in action!

Your Voice Matters

Even though kids can't vote yet, your voice still matters—and one day, you'll have the power to help shape the future of your town, state, and country.

Here are ways **young people** can start getting involved:

- **Learn how government works** and pay attention to current events.

- **Talk about issues** that matter to you with friends, family, and teachers.

- **Visit government buildings**, museums, and civic centers to see leadership in action.

- **Write letters** to local leaders to share your ideas and concerns.

And when you **turn 18**, you'll be able to **register to vote** and take part in elections. Voting is one of the most powerful ways to **make your voice heard** and help your community.

In Pennsylvania, **voting is a tradition** that goes all the way back to William Penn's colony. Whether it's choosing a mayor, state senator, or even the next president, every vote counts.

A State That Shaped a Nation

Pennsylvania's role in government is nothing short of amazing. From the first democratic ideas of William Penn, to the signing of the Declaration and Constitution, to today's Capitol debates and elections, this state has **led the way in standing up for rights, fairness, and freedom**.

So the next time you walk through Philadelphia or drive past Harrisburg, remember—you're not just passing buildings. You're walking through **living history**, where democracy was born and where it continues to grow every day.

And someday, **you** could be one of the people helping lead Pennsylvania into the future!

Chapter 9: The Amish and Pennsylvania Dutch Country

One of the most unique and fascinating parts of Pennsylvania is the peaceful world of **Amish Country**. Here, you'll find a community that seems frozen in time—where people ride in horse-drawn buggies, wear plain clothing, and live without electricity or modern technology. This way of life may seem very different, but it's all part of their deep traditions and strong beliefs.

Welcome to **Pennsylvania Dutch Country**, where the pace is slower, the values are rooted in faith and simplicity, and every visit feels like stepping into a living history book.

Who Are the Amish?

The **Amish** are a religious group known for living simply and apart from the modern world. Their ancestors came to Pennsylvania in the **1700s**, mostly from **Germany and Switzerland**, in search of **religious freedom**. William Penn's colony welcomed them, and they quickly built farms and communities that still exist today.

Amish beliefs come from the **Anabaptist Christian tradition**, which emphasizes:

- **Living humbly and simply**

- **Hard work and community**

- **Peace and nonviolence**

- **Separation from the world** (meaning they avoid modern technology and pop culture)

In daily life, this means:

- Amish families **don't use electricity from the power grid**

- They travel by **horse and buggy** instead of cars

- They wear **plain clothing**—often black, white, or blue—and avoid flashy patterns or buttons

- Most Amish children only go to school until **8th grade**, learning mainly reading, writing, math, and farming skills

Even though they live differently, the Amish are kind, generous, and deeply rooted in values that have stayed the same for centuries.

Farming and Craftsmanship

The Amish are famous for their **strong work ethic**, especially in **farming, building, and crafting**.

- **Farming** is a way of life. They grow crops like corn, wheat, and alfalfa, and raise animals like cows, chickens, and horses. Many Amish farms are **completely self-sufficient**, meaning they grow what they eat and use what they build.

- A **barn raising** is one of the most amazing Amish traditions. When a family needs a new barn, the entire community comes together to **build it in a single day!** Everyone has a job—men work on the frame, women prepare meals, and kids help wherever they can.

- Amish people are also talented **woodworkers and quilters**. Their **handmade furniture** is beautifully crafted and built to last for generations. Their **quilts** feature colorful patterns and are sewn entirely by hand, often as gifts or for fundraising auctions.

- You'll often see **roadside stands** where Amish families sell fresh vegetables, baked goods, and crafts. These stands usually run on the honor system—meaning you leave your payment in a jar and make your own change!

Visiting Amish Country

One of the best ways to learn about the Amish is to **visit Lancaster County**, the heart of Amish Country in Pennsylvania. It's just a few hours from Philadelphia and offers a mix of **rural beauty, delicious food, and cultural experiences**.

Things to see and do:

- **Ride in a real horse-drawn buggy** through scenic farmland

- Visit a **working Amish farm**, where you can pet animals, see crops, and learn how they live

- Explore **Amish markets**, full of homemade jellies, warm pretzels, and fresh pies

- Watch demonstrations of **quilt-making, candle-dipping, or furniture building**

When visiting, it's important to **respect Amish customs**:

- Amish people generally **do not like to be photographed**, as they believe it's prideful or against their beliefs

- Be polite and friendly, but don't try to push them to explain or change their lifestyle

- Learn by observing, asking respectful questions, or taking guided tours with local experts

Experiencing Amish life firsthand helps kids understand that **different ways of living can still share the same values**—like kindness, hard work, and family.

Pennsylvania Dutch Language and Culture

The term "**Pennsylvania Dutch**" can be a little confusing. It doesn't mean people are from the Netherlands—it actually comes from the word **"Deutsch,"** which means "German." So,

Pennsylvania Dutch people are mostly of **German and Swiss heritage**.

This culture includes both **Amish and Mennonite communities**, along with other groups who speak a version of **German dialect** and keep traditional customs alive.

Fun parts of Pennsylvania Dutch culture include:

- **Language**: While most Amish speak **English**, many also speak **Pennsylvania German** or "Deitsch" at home and in worship.

- **Foods**: Don't miss out on **shoofly pie** (a sweet molasses pie), **chow-chow** (a pickled vegetable mix), and **scrapple** (a breakfast meat made from pork scraps and cornmeal). It might sound strange, but many of these foods are surprisingly tasty!

- **Festivals and traditions**: From **quilt shows** to **harvest celebrations**, the Pennsylvania Dutch love to gather as a community and celebrate their heritage.

You might also hear old-fashioned expressions like:

- "Make wet?" = Are you going to wash the dishes?

- "Throw your hat in the creek" = Give up! These sayings come from a blend of German and English, and they add flavor to the culture.

A Simple Life, a Strong Community

The Amish and Pennsylvania Dutch way of life may seem unusual at first, but it's filled with meaning. They remind us that **you don't need the latest gadgets or flashy things to live a full, happy life**. Their focus on **faith, family, and community** helps them stay strong and connected—even in a fast-changing world.

Visiting Pennsylvania Dutch Country is like entering a peaceful, thoughtful world that's both old-fashioned and full of heart. And whether you're admiring a hand-sewn quilt or waving at a horse-drawn buggy, you'll come away with a deeper appreciation for the many different ways people live in Pennsylvania.

Chapter 10: Pennsylvania's Incredible Inventions

Did you know that many of the things we use, eat, or enjoy every day were invented or developed right in Pennsylvania? From life-saving medical breakthroughs to fun toys and tasty treats, the Keystone State has a long history of creativity and innovation. Inventors, scientists, and dreamers have turned their big ideas into real-life products that changed the world.

Let's take a closer look at the amazing inventions and industries that started in Pennsylvania—and how they continue to impact our lives today.

Everyday Items Made in Pennsylvania

Some of the simplest things we use every day were first created or made famous right here in Pennsylvania. You might be surprised by how many of them you recognize!

- **The Pencil**
  While pencils were used in other parts of the world, the first **mass-produced American pencil** was made in **Philadelphia**. Factories there helped turn pencils into a common tool for writing, drawing, and learning.

- **The Slinky**
  This **iconic toy** was invented in **1943 by Richard James**, a naval engineer from Pennsylvania. He was working with springs when one fell off a shelf and "walked" down. The Slinky was born! It became one of the best-selling toys of all time—and it's still made in PA

today.

- **Bubble Gum**
  In **1928**, a man named **Walter Diemer** invented bubble gum at the **Fleer Chewing Gum Company** in **Philadelphia**. He was experimenting with gum recipes and stumbled upon a formula that stretched and popped—perfect for blowing bubbles!

It's amazing how these everyday items started as simple ideas and became household favorites around the world.

Major Breakthroughs

Not all inventions are toys and snacks—some of Pennsylvania's contributions have saved lives and changed the world forever.

- **The Polio Vaccine**
  In the 1950s, a deadly disease called **polio** was spreading quickly and paralyzing thousands of children. A scientist named **Jonas Salk**, working at the **University of Pittsburgh**, developed the first successful **polio vaccine**. This breakthrough nearly wiped out the disease and is considered one of the greatest medical achievements of the 20th century.

- **First Commercial Radio Station**
  In **1920**, Pittsburgh became home to **KDKA**, the **first commercial radio station** in the United States. The first broadcast? The results of the presidential election! This marked the beginning of **radio news, music, and**

entertainment, which later led to TV and modern media.

Thanks to brilliant Pennsylvanians, the state has contributed not just to fun and convenience—but to health, communication, and human progress.

Tasty Inventions

Pennsylvania is also a dreamland for people with a sweet tooth. Some of America's most popular candies and treats were born here!

- **Hershey's Chocolate**
  Perhaps the most famous treat to come out of Pennsylvania is **Hershey's chocolate**. In the town of **Hershey, PA**, Milton Hershey built a factory and an entire community for his workers. He created the first **mass-produced milk chocolate bar** in America and made chocolate affordable for everyone—not just the rich.
  Today, Hershey's makes chocolate bars, kisses, syrup, and more—and the town is known as **"The Sweetest Place on Earth."** You can even visit **Hersheypark**, a theme park with roller coasters and chocolate fun!

- **Peeps Marshmallows**
  Those brightly colored marshmallow chicks and bunnies you see at Easter? They're called **Peeps**, and they're made by **Just Born**, a company based in **Bethlehem, Pennsylvania**. They started in the 1950s and now come in all kinds of shapes, colors, and even

flavors!

Pennsylvania is full of delicious history—and it's still cooking up sweet new ideas every day.

Tech and Transportation

Pennsylvania didn't just invent cool things—it helped **build America's infrastructure**, powering industries and transportation systems that shaped the country.

- **Railroad Growth**
  The invention and expansion of **railroads** changed the way people traveled and how goods were shipped. Pennsylvania was at the heart of this revolution. Cities like **Altoona** became famous for their **rail yards and engineering**, and the **Pennsylvania Railroad** became one of the biggest and most powerful rail systems in the world.

  Kids can still visit places like the **Railroad Museum of Pennsylvania** in Strasburg, where you can see **real train engines** and learn how they worked.

- **Bethlehem Steel**
  In the city of **Bethlehem**, one of the most important companies in American history was born—**Bethlehem Steel**. This company helped produce the steel used to build **bridges, skyscrapers, ships, and railroads** all over the country.
  Bethlehem Steel also supplied the U.S. military with materials during both World Wars, playing a major role

61

in America's success.

Even though the steel mills have shut down, you can still visit **SteelStacks**, a modern arts and culture center built on the old factory site. It's a cool example of how Pennsylvania's industrial past is still part of its future.

The Spirit of Invention Lives On

Pennsylvania has always been a place where **big ideas take shape**. Whether it's a toy that tumbles down stairs, a life-saving vaccine, or a sweet chocolate treat, the state's inventors and innovators have helped shape the modern world in ways both big and small.

And here's the best part—**the next great invention could come from you!** Whether you're sketching a design, asking big questions, or taking things apart to see how they work, you're following in the footsteps of the many brilliant Pennsylvanians who dreamed something up and made it real.

So keep your eyes open, stay curious, and never stop imagining. You never know where the next great idea will come from—but Pennsylvania has proven it could start in the most unexpected places.

Chapter 11: Food Favorites from the Keystone State

If there's one thing Pennsylvania does right (besides history and nature), it's **food**. The Keystone State is home to mouthwatering dishes, legendary desserts, and snack brands that people across the country recognize instantly. Whether it's something sizzling off the grill, baked from scratch, or straight from a roadside stand, Pennsylvania's food is as rich and diverse as its people.

Let's dig in and explore the delicious favorites that make Pennsylvania one tasty place to be!

Savory Classics

Pennsylvania has a few famous foods that you simply *have* to try if you visit the state. These savory staples are full of flavor—and full of local pride.

- **Philly Cheesesteak**
  Probably the most iconic food in Pennsylvania, the Philly cheesesteak was invented in—you guessed it—**Philadelphia**. It's made with thinly sliced beef, melted cheese (usually Cheez Whiz, provolone, or American), and grilled onions on a long hoagie roll.
  Locals will tell you there's a right way to order it: "Whiz wit" means Cheez Whiz with onions. Don't forget to try famous spots like **Pat's** and **Geno's**—and prepare for a debate about which one is better!

- **Pierogies**
  These doughy dumplings are stuffed with fillings like

potatoes and cheese, **sauerkraut**, or **meat**. Pierogies came to Pennsylvania with Eastern European immigrants and became especially popular in places like **Pittsburgh**. They're usually boiled and then fried in butter and onions until golden and delicious.

- **Hoagies**
  Known in other places as subs or grinders, hoagies are **stacked sandwiches** made on long rolls with deli meats, cheese, lettuce, tomatoes, onions, and dressings. Originating in Philadelphia, hoagies are a lunchtime favorite—and every local deli has their own special version.

These savory dishes are more than just meals—they're part of Pennsylvania's identity.

Sweet Treats

If you've got a sweet tooth, you're in for a treat—Pennsylvania is home to some of the most satisfying desserts and snacks around.

- **Shoofly Pie**
  A classic Pennsylvania Dutch dessert made with **molasses and brown sugar**, this pie has a gooey bottom layer and a crumbly topping. It gets its funny name because the sweet smell was said to **attract flies**, and bakers would have to "shoo" them away!

- **Whoopie Pies**
  These dessert sandwiches are made from two soft

chocolate cakes with a creamy filling in the middle. Whoopie pies are believed to have originated with **Amish bakers**, and their name comes from the joyful "whoopie!" shouted when they were found in lunchboxes.

- **Tastykakes**
  These snack cakes are made by a company in **Philadelphia** and are a lunchtime favorite for many kids across the state. Varieties include **Kandy Kakes, Butterscotch Krimpets, and Peanut Butter Tandy Cakes**—each with its own fan club.

In Pennsylvania, dessert is not an afterthought—it's a proud tradition.

Pennsylvania Dutch Dishes

Some of the most unique and flavorful foods in the state come from **Pennsylvania Dutch Country**, where Amish and Mennonite communities have kept culinary traditions alive for generations.

- **Scrapple**
  This breakfast dish might sound strange at first—it's made from pork scraps, cornmeal, and spices, shaped into a loaf, and then sliced and fried until crispy. But it's beloved by many Pennsylvanians and is usually served with eggs and syrup or ketchup.

- **Chicken Pot Pie (PA Dutch Style)**
  This isn't your typical pie with a crust. In Pennsylvania

Dutch cooking, chicken pot pie is more like a **thick soup** made with **boiled chicken, potatoes, vegetables, and wide square noodles**. It's hearty, comforting, and totally different from the baked version you might expect.

- **Apple Butter, chow-chow, and corn fritters**
  Other favorites include sweet **apple butter** spread on warm bread, **chow-chow** (a tangy mix of pickled vegetables), and **corn fritters**, which are fried and golden on the outside, soft on the inside.

These dishes show how Pennsylvania Dutch families have turned simple ingredients into memorable meals for centuries.

Local Snacks and Drinks

Even the snacks and drinks you find in convenience stores in Pennsylvania can be a special experience!

- **Herr's Chips**
  Based in **Nottingham, PA**, Herr's makes a wide variety of **potato chips and snacks** in flavors like **barbecue, sour cream & onion, dill pickle, and even Old Bay seasoning**. They've been a snack staple since 1946 and even offer factory tours!

- **Birch Beer**
  A cousin of root beer, birch beer is a **sweet, fizzy drink** made from birch tree bark. It comes in red, brown, and clear varieties and has a slightly minty, vanilla-like flavor. You'll often find it at Amish markets and

small-town festivals.

- **PA Maple Syrup**
  In northern Pennsylvania, **maple trees** are tapped in early spring to produce **fresh maple syrup**. This golden syrup is perfect on pancakes, waffles, or even drizzled on vanilla ice cream. Some towns even host **maple festivals** to celebrate the harvest.

These local snacks and sips show off the flavors that are uniquely Pennsylvania—and they make every meal (or road trip) more fun.

A State Full of Flavor

Whether you're biting into a warm whoopie pie, sipping birch beer, or trying scrapple for the first time, Pennsylvania's foods tell the story of its **culture, history, and people**. Each dish has a tale behind it—whether it comes from immigrant traditions, Amish kitchens, or creative inventors with a sweet tooth.

From farm stands to city food trucks, the Keystone State is one big buffet of savory bites and sweet delights. So grab a plate and enjoy—because in Pennsylvania, every meal is a chance to explore!

Chapter 12: Pennsylvania's Sports Scene

Pennsylvania is more than just history, chocolate, and natural beauty—it's also a state that **lives and breathes sports**. Whether it's packed professional stadiums, roaring college crowds, or high school rivalries under the Friday night lights, sports are a huge part of life in the Keystone State.

From the NFL to Little League, from cheering in the stands to playing on the field, sports in Pennsylvania bring people together and create memories that last a lifetime. Let's take a look at what makes Pennsylvania's sports scene so exciting!

Professional Teams

Pennsylvania is home to some of the most **passionate and loyal sports fans** in the country. The state has **six major professional teams** that represent it in football, baseball, hockey, and basketball—and their fans are proud, loud, and serious about winning.

- **Philadelphia Eagles (NFL)**
  Known as the "Birds," the Eagles are based in **Philadelphia** and have a huge following across eastern Pennsylvania. Their fans fill **Lincoln Financial Field** every Sunday in the fall, dressed in green and white and chanting "Fly, Eagles, Fly!"
  They won their first **Super Bowl** in 2018, and the celebration took over the city for days.

- **Pittsburgh Steelers (NFL)**
  On the other side of the state, the Steelers are just as

beloved. They've won **six Super Bowl championships**, tying for the most in NFL history. Their stadium, **Acrisure Stadium**, fills with fans waving **Terrible Towels**—bright yellow rally towels that have become a symbol of Pittsburgh pride.

- **Philadelphia Phillies (MLB)**
  The Phillies are the **oldest continuous, one-name, one-city team** in American pro sports. They've been around since 1883 and play at **Citizens Bank Park**. They've won **two World Series titles**, and fans love their mix of tradition and toughness.

- **Pittsburgh Pirates (MLB)**
  The Pirates, also known as the "Bucs," play at **PNC Park**, one of the most scenic stadiums in baseball, with a view of downtown Pittsburgh. The team has **five World Series championships** in its history.

- **Philadelphia 76ers (NBA)**
  The "Sixers" are one of the oldest basketball teams in the NBA. They've had legendary players like **Wilt Chamberlain, Julius Erving (Dr. J), and Allen Iverson**. Today, the team is known for their slogan: **"Trust the Process."**

- **Pittsburgh Penguins (NHL)**
  The Penguins are a powerhouse hockey team with multiple **Stanley Cup** wins. Their mascot, **Iceburgh**, is a hit with kids, and the team has had superstars like **Sidney Crosby and Mario Lemieux**.

Whether you're cheering for a Philly or Pittsburgh team, you're part of a **state with sports in its DNA**.

College Pride

It's not just the pros who get all the love. Pennsylvania is also home to **powerhouse college teams** that fire up student sections and entire communities.

- **Penn State University (Nittany Lions)**
  Located in **State College**, Penn State's football team plays in **Beaver Stadium**, one of the largest stadiums in the world. Game days bring more than **100,000 fans** in blue and white, and the **White Out** game—where everyone wears white—is a sight to behold.

- **University of Pittsburgh (Pitt Panthers)**
  The Panthers are longtime rivals of Penn State and play their games in **Pittsburgh**. Pitt's football and basketball teams have strong fan bases, and their battles with schools like **West Virginia** and **Syracuse** are intense.

- **Temple University (Owls)**
  Based in **Philadelphia**, Temple has a proud history in both football and basketball. The Owls have produced top athletes and draw big crowds, especially during basketball season.

College games in Pennsylvania aren't just games—they're **traditions** full of marching bands, tailgates, chants, and school spirit that lasts a lifetime.

Youth and School Sports

All across Pennsylvania, kids lace up their cleats, shoot hoops, swing bats, and learn about **teamwork, determination, and sportsmanship.**

- **Friday Night Lights**
  High school football is huge in many towns. On Friday nights in the fall, **entire communities gather** under the lights to cheer on their local teams. Marching bands perform, cheerleaders energize the crowd, and players give it their all on the field.

- **Other School Sports**
  Beyond football, Pennsylvania schools offer everything from **soccer and basketball to wrestling, track, and swimming.** Local rivalries between schools can be just as intense as the pros, with students and parents packing the stands.

- **Youth Leagues**
  Whether it's **Little League Baseball**, **rec basketball**, or **youth hockey**, thousands of kids in Pennsylvania grow up playing sports. These leagues teach skills, build friendships, and create memories that last long after the final whistle.

Sports are a big part of **growing up in Pennsylvania**—win or lose, it's all about giving your best and having fun.

Fun Facts and Rivalries

Sports fans in Pennsylvania don't just love the game—they live for **rivalries**. The state is practically **divided down the middle** between the east (Philadelphia) and the west (Pittsburgh), and that leads to some friendly (and not-so-friendly) battles.

- **Eagles vs. Steelers**
  While these teams don't play each other often, when they do, it's a **statewide showdown**. Families might even be split—Mom cheering for the Steelers, Dad rooting for the Eagles. It's a classic **"house divided"** situation.

- **College Rivalries**

    - **Penn State vs. Pitt** is a historic matchup that goes back over 100 years. When these two meet, the game is full of passion and pride.

    - **Temple vs. Villanova** and **La Salle vs. Saint Joseph's** are some of the classic **Philadelphia basketball rivalries**, especially in a city that lives and breathes hoops.

- **Pittsburgh vs. Philadelphia Everything**
  From hockey (Penguins vs. Flyers) to baseball (Pirates vs. Phillies), there's always a little extra fire when teams from the two big cities go head-to-head.

And here's a fun fact: the **Little League World Series**, one of the biggest youth baseball tournaments in the world, is held every year in **Williamsport, Pennsylvania!**

Sports Bring Pennsylvania Together

Whether you're waving a Terrible Towel, cheering in a student section, or playing catch in your backyard, sports are a huge part of life in Pennsylvania. They teach us **teamwork, perseverance, and pride**, and they help bring people of all ages and backgrounds together.

So grab your jersey, find your seat, and get ready to shout and cheer—because in Pennsylvania, **every day is game day**.

Chapter 13: Art, Music, and Culture Across the State

Pennsylvania isn't just about battlefields and sports—it's also a state bursting with **creativity, expression, and celebration**. From world-famous art museums to toe-tapping music festivals, Pennsylvania's cultural scene is full of color and life. Whether you're into paintings, plays, jazz, hip-hop, or parades, there's something for everyone to explore and enjoy.

Let's take a closer look at the artistic heart of the Keystone State.

Visual Art and Museums

Pennsylvania is home to **incredible art museums**, galleries, and public installations that let you **see the world through a different lens**.

- **Philadelphia Museum of Art**
  This world-famous museum isn't just filled with masterpieces—it's also famous for its **front steps**, known as the **"Rocky Steps."** Visitors from all over the world run up them just like the movie boxer **Rocky Balboa** did. Inside, you'll find paintings, sculptures, and artifacts from around the globe—including ancient armor, impressionist paintings, and modern art.

- **The Andy Warhol Museum (Pittsburgh)**
  This museum is dedicated to **Andy Warhol**, one of the most famous pop artists in history, and a native of Pittsburgh. Warhol's bold, colorful work included paintings of soup cans, celebrities, and everyday

objects. The museum is filled with his original artwork, personal items, and interactive exhibits that let you dive into the world of pop art.

- **Smaller Art Spaces**
  From the **Lancaster Museum of Art** to **community galleries in Erie and Bethlehem**, Pennsylvania is filled with places that support local artists. Many small towns even host **art walks and festivals**, where painters, photographers, and sculptors show off their work.

Art in Pennsylvania isn't just something you look at—it's something you experience.

Music from All Styles

Pennsylvania is a **melting pot of musical styles**, and its cities and towns have produced some of the **biggest names in the industry**. From classical concerts to indie coffeehouse shows, the state's music scene is diverse and lively.

- **Classical Music**
  The **Philadelphia Orchestra** is one of the best in the world and performs at the **Kimmel Center**. Young music lovers can enjoy student concerts, youth orchestra performances, and holiday shows.

- **Hip-Hop and R&B**
  Philadelphia helped launch the careers of artists like **Will Smith**, **Boyz II Men**, and **Meek Mill**. Their sounds helped shape music across the country.

- **Folk and Americana**
  In smaller towns and mountain regions, you'll hear the sounds of **banjos, fiddles, and acoustic guitars.** Folk festivals like the **Philadelphia Folk Festival** celebrate these traditional styles.

- **Indie and Rock**
  Bands and solo artists from cities like Pittsburgh and Allentown are part of the state's growing **indie music scene.** You'll find live music in cafes, record stores, and summer block parties all over the state.

Whether you like loud guitars, quiet violins, or catchy beats, there's always a new tune to discover in Pennsylvania.

Big Names and Local Legends

Some of the world's most recognizable musicians, actors, and artists got their start in Pennsylvania:

- **Taylor Swift**, born in Reading, went from singing country songs to becoming one of the biggest pop stars in the world.

- **Tina Fey**, from Upper Darby, became a comedy legend on *Saturday Night Live* and in movies.

- **Jeff Goldblum**, the quirky and cool actor from *Jurassic Park*, grew up in West Homestead, near Pittsburgh.

- **Patti LaBelle**, the "Godmother of Soul," got her start in Philadelphia.

And it's not just the famous faces—Pennsylvania is full of **local legends**, street performers, and rising stars. Many musicians and actors perform in their hometowns, helping to build strong creative communities.

Theater and Performances

Lights, curtains, action! Pennsylvania has a rich **theater tradition**, from grand stages to cozy community shows.

- **Walnut Street Theatre (Philadelphia)**
  This is the **oldest continuously operating theater in the United States**. Opened in 1809, it has hosted presidents, famous actors, and countless classic plays. Today, it offers a mix of musicals, comedies, and dramas that kids and adults alike can enjoy.

- **Community Playhouses**
  Almost every corner of the state has a **community theater group** putting on plays and musicals throughout the year. These performances are often made up of local volunteers, including kids and teens.

- **Outdoor Theater and Summer Shows**
  When the weather warms up, Pennsylvania hosts **outdoor performances** in parks and amphitheaters. Whether it's Shakespeare under the stars or a kid-friendly fairy tale, these shows are fun, affordable,

and a great way to spend a summer evening.

Acting, singing, and storytelling are big parts of Pennsylvania's cultural scene—and they're for everyone to enjoy or join in!

Cultural Celebrations

Pennsylvania's culture is shaped by people from **all over the world**, and their heritage is celebrated through **festivals, parades, and special events**.

- **Greek Festivals**
  Towns like **York** and **Reading** host colorful Greek festivals with **dancing, music, and delicious food** like gyros and baklava.

- **Italian Festivals**
  Cities like **Scranton and Philadelphia** celebrate Italian heritage with events like the **St. Anthony's Festival**, full of food stands, live bands, and family fun.

- **Puerto Rican Day Parade (Philadelphia)**
  This joyful celebration features **colorful costumes, traditional music, and dance performances** that honor Puerto Rican pride and culture.

- **Juneteenth Events**
  Celebrated on **June 19th**, Juneteenth marks the end of slavery in the United States. Communities across Pennsylvania hold **festivals, history events, and parades** to recognize African-American heritage and

the ongoing fight for equality.

From **Chinese New Year celebrations** in Pittsburgh to **Diwali festivals** in central PA, the state's many communities show that Pennsylvania's strength is in its **diversity**.

A State Full of Creative Spirit

Pennsylvania's art, music, and culture shine in every corner of the state—from the steps of an art museum to the stage of a school play, from classical symphonies to backyard rock bands.

No matter where you go, you'll find **people creating, performing, and sharing their stories**. And whether you're in the audience or up on stage, you're part of the show too.

So dance, draw, sing, clap, and cheer—because in Pennsylvania, **creativity is everywhere**, and everyone's invited to join in!

Chapter 14: Cool Science and Tech in Pennsylvania

Pennsylvania might be famous for its history, chocolate, and sports—but it's also a state bursting with **science, technology, and discovery**. From kid-friendly science museums to dinosaur fossils and high-tech medical research, there's no shortage of hands-on learning and cutting-edge exploration happening all across the Keystone State.

Whether you're dreaming of becoming a doctor, astronaut, geologist, or engineer, Pennsylvania has exciting places and stories that will spark your curiosity and imagination.

Hands-On Science Fun

In Pennsylvania, science isn't just something you read about—it's something you **do**. There are incredible museums and centers where kids can **touch, build, explore, and experiment**.

- **The Franklin Institute (Philadelphia)**
  Named after the legendary inventor and scientist **Benjamin Franklin**, this museum is packed with fun, interactive exhibits. You can:

    - Crawl through a **giant human heart**

    - Control air pressure to launch rockets

    - Create electricity by pedaling a bike

- o Watch live science shows and visit the on-site planetarium

- It's the perfect place for hands-on fun while learning about physics, biology, and chemistry.

- **Carnegie Science Center (Pittsburgh)**
  Located on the banks of the Ohio River, this science center is full of excitement for curious minds. Highlights include:

  - o The **roboworld** exhibit with robots you can program

  - o A **space station simulation**

  - o A **four-story-high movie screen**

  - o **SportsWorks**, where you explore the science behind movement and athletics
    Plus, you can even **tour a real submarine**, the USS Requin!

- **Da Vinci Science Center (Allentown)**
  Especially great for younger kids, this museum includes experiments with **magnets, motion, sound, light**, and more. It also has a creative play area and science-themed activities to inspire future inventors and engineers.

Pennsylvania's science centers make learning exciting and fun—and they're great places for field trips, birthday parties, or weekend adventures.

Natural Science and Wildlife

Beyond city museums, Pennsylvania's great outdoors is full of **scientific wonders**, from ancient fossils to live wildlife.

- **Dinosaur Fossils**
  While most dinosaur bones are found out west, Pennsylvania has its own slice of dino history. Fossil beds have revealed ancient **footprints and plant life**, showing how different the state looked millions of years ago. You can explore prehistoric exhibits at places like the **State Museum of Pennsylvania** in Harrisburg.

- **Geology and Rocks**
  The Appalachian Mountains are filled with cool rocks and minerals. In central and western PA, you can find **coal, limestone, quartz**, and even small **crystals**. Geology clubs and nature centers help kids learn how these rocks formed and how they've shaped the landscape.

- **Wildlife Centers**
  Pennsylvania's forests and parks are full of amazing animals—like **white-tailed deer, bald eagles, black bears, and red foxes**. Wildlife centers and sanctuaries help protect animals and teach kids about conservation. You can visit places like:

  - **Hawk Mountain Sanctuary** for birdwatching

  - **Shaver's Creek Environmental Center** for nature trails and animal talks

- ZooAmerica in Hershey for learning about North American wildlife

From fossils to forests, Pennsylvania is a natural classroom for anyone who loves Earth science and the environment.

Pennsylvania's Role in Space and Medicine

It might surprise you to learn that Pennsylvania has deep connections to **outer space and modern medicine**.

- **NASA Connections**
  The state is home to companies and universities that work with **NASA** on aerospace technology. For example:

  - **Drexel University** and **Carnegie Mellon University** have partnered on **robotics and space missions**.

  - The **NASA Pennsylvania Space Grant Consortium** supports space education and research at colleges and schools across the state.

- Pennsylvania scientists have worked on everything from **spacesuit materials to moon rovers**, making space dreams a reality.

- **Medical Research and Hospitals**
  Pennsylvania is also a leader in **medical science and healthcare**. Some of the country's top hospitals and

research centers are located here, including:

- **University of Pennsylvania Health System** (Philadelphia)

- **UPMC** (University of Pittsburgh Medical Center)

- **Children's Hospital of Philadelphia (CHOP)**—one of the best pediatric hospitals in the world

- These institutions are working on **cancer treatments, vaccines, gene therapy**, and more. In fact, many of the **COVID-19 vaccine breakthroughs** were researched in labs in Pennsylvania.

From outer space to inner health, the state is at the forefront of discovery.

Energy and Industry

Pennsylvania has a long history of helping **power the country**, and it's still leading in **energy and innovation** today.

- **Coal**
  Pennsylvania was once the top coal-producing state in the nation. **Anthracite coal**, a hard and clean-burning type, came from **northeastern PA** and helped power factories and trains during the Industrial Revolution.

- **Fracking and Natural Gas**
  In modern times, the state has become a major

producer of **natural gas** through a method called **hydraulic fracturing**, or "fracking." It's controversial, with debates over energy needs vs. environmental protection.

- **Wind and Solar Energy**
  Pennsylvania is working toward cleaner energy, too! **Wind farms** in the mountains and **solar panel farms** are popping up across the state to provide **renewable power**.

- **The Oil Boom in Titusville**
  Did you know that the world's **first commercial oil well** was drilled in **Titusville, Pennsylvania**, in 1859? That discovery kicked off the **global oil industry** and turned Pennsylvania into a hub for fuel and innovation.

  Today, you can visit the **Drake Well Museum** in Titusville to see where it all began and learn about the **history of oil drilling** and how it changed the world.

The Spirit of Discovery

Science and technology are **alive and thriving** in Pennsylvania. Whether you're building a robot, studying the stars, hiking through fossil-filled forests, or learning how energy powers your home, you're tapping into the same curiosity that has inspired Pennsylvania inventors, doctors, and explorers for generations.

And who knows? Someday, *you* might be the one making a discovery, launching a spacecraft, or inventing a life-saving medicine—right here in the state where science never stops moving forward.

Chapter 15: Awesome Places to Visit

From thrilling roller coasters to historic landmarks and natural wonders, Pennsylvania is packed with places that make **perfect adventures for kids and families**. Whether you love exciting rides, cool museums, exploring the great outdoors, or discovering how your favorite snacks are made, the Keystone State has something just for you.

Let's take a look at some of the **most awesome places to visit** in Pennsylvania—you might want to start packing your bags!

Theme Parks and Kid Attractions

If you're looking for **fun, laughter, and a little adrenaline**, Pennsylvania is home to some of the best family-friendly theme parks in the country.

- **Hersheypark (Hershey, PA)**
  This chocolate-themed park was originally built for Hershey's factory workers, but today it's a **world-class amusement park** with over 70 rides, including wild roller coasters and gentle kiddie rides. Plus, you can visit **Chocolate World** to learn how chocolate is made—and even create your own candy bar!

- **Dorney Park & Wildwater Kingdom (Allentown, PA)**
  A combo amusement and water park, Dorney Park has everything from twisty coasters to lazy rivers. It's great for families who want **thrills and splashes** all in one day.

- **Dutch Wonderland (Lancaster, PA)**
  Designed especially for **young children**, this fairy
  tale-themed park includes friendly rides, live shows, a
  water play area, and lots of interactive attractions. It's a
  great place for first-time amusement park visitors.

Pennsylvania knows how to deliver **nonstop fun**—and these
parks are sure to bring out smiles.

Historic Must-Sees

Pennsylvania is also full of **incredible places where history
comes alive**. These sites are not just educational—they're fun
to explore and full of surprises.

- **The Liberty Bell (Philadelphia, PA)**
  One of the most famous symbols of freedom in the
  world, the Liberty Bell is housed in its own pavilion next
  to Independence Hall. It's cracked, but still proudly on
  display for millions of visitors each year.

- **Independence Hall (Philadelphia, PA)**
  The **Declaration of Independence** and **U.S.
  Constitution** were debated and signed here. You can
  take a tour and stand in the very room where America
  was born.

- **Eastern State Penitentiary (Philadelphia, PA)**
  Once one of the most advanced prisons in the world,
  this spooky and fascinating historic site lets visitors walk
  through cellblocks, learn about prison history, and even
  explore haunted parts during Halloween events. Kids

will love the mystery and stories behind the towering stone walls.

These sites prove that **history can be just as exciting as a roller coaster**—especially when you're standing where it all happened.

Railroad and Mining Museums

All aboard! Pennsylvania played a huge role in the history of **trains and coal**, and you can still **ride the rails and explore mines** today.

- **Railroad Museum of Pennsylvania (Strasburg, PA)**
  Home to dozens of real train engines and rail cars, this museum is a dream for train lovers. You can even climb aboard many of the locomotives, see how they worked, and learn how railroads shaped the country.

- **Steamtown National Historic Site (Scranton, PA)**
  A working rail yard with **steam engine demonstrations**, museum exhibits, and even **train rides**! It's run by the National Park Service and gives kids a hands-on experience with how trains moved people and goods across the country.

- **Lackawanna Coal Mine Tour (Scranton, PA)**
  Want to ride an old mining car **300 feet underground** into a real coal mine? This tour lets you experience what life was like for miners—and teaches you about one of Pennsylvania's most important industries.

From whistles and coal dust to tracks and tunnels, these places are full of **engineering marvels and real-life adventure**.

Nature Escapes

Pennsylvania's wild side is full of **natural beauty and peaceful places** perfect for hiking, camping, or just getting away from it all.

- **Pennsylvania Grand Canyon (Tioga County, PA)**
  Officially known as **Pine Creek Gorge**, this breathtaking canyon stretches for 47 miles and offers **stunning views, waterfalls, and wildlife**. There are scenic overlooks, hiking trails, and even horse-drawn wagon rides in the summer.

- **Ricketts Glen State Park (Benton, PA)**
  Famous for its **22 waterfalls**, this park is a favorite for hikers and nature photographers. You can hike the **Falls Trail**, picnic by the lake, or camp under the stars.

- **Allegheny National Forest**
  Located in northwest PA, this massive forest is full of **hiking trails, campgrounds, rivers, and wildlife**. It's a peaceful place to unplug and enjoy the great outdoors.

Whether you're climbing a rocky trail, splashing in a stream, or spotting a bald eagle, Pennsylvania's nature spots are perfect for **family adventures and outdoor fun**.

Off-the-Beaten-Path Fun

Some of Pennsylvania's coolest places aren't the most famous—they're the ones full of **surprises and hands-on activities** you won't find anywhere else.

- **Crayola Experience (Easton, PA)**
  If you love art, this colorful attraction is a must-see. Inside, you can **create your own crayon**, watch crayons being made, design digital art, and explore dozens of creative stations. It's a dream come true for crafty kids!

- **Turkey Hill Experience (Columbia, PA)**
  Ever wondered how **ice cream and iced tea** are made? This interactive factory experience lets you **taste-test products**, design your own flavor, milk mechanical cows, and learn about dairy farming. Yum!

- **Knoebels Amusement Resort (Elysburg, PA)**
  This **family-owned amusement park** is special for one major reason: **admission is free!** You only pay for the rides you want to go on, which makes it a great budget-friendly option. Knoebels has a classic vibe, wooden roller coasters, a swimming area, and even camping spots nearby.

These unique destinations show that **big fun sometimes comes in unexpected packages.**

Ready to Explore?

Pennsylvania is bursting with places that are **fun, exciting, and unforgettable**. Whether you're racing down a roller coaster, making your own crayon, exploring a dark coal mine, or gazing into a giant canyon, the state is full of **kid-friendly adventures** that teach, entertain, and inspire.

So next time you're looking for somewhere cool to visit, remember: you don't have to leave Pennsylvania to find **awesome attractions, amazing stories, and epic memories** waiting to be made.

Chapter 16: The Changing Seasons and PA Weather

One of the most magical things about living in or visiting Pennsylvania is getting to experience **all four seasons** in full color, sound, and feeling. The state has cold, snowy winters, warm and sunny summers, blooming springs, and fall seasons that are so colorful, they look like paintings. Each season brings its own kind of beauty—and its own kinds of weather and activities.

Let's explore what Pennsylvania's seasons are like and how the weather shapes everything from your clothes to the forests, from sports to animal behavior!

What to Expect Each Season

Pennsylvania is in the **northeastern United States**, which means it has a **temperate climate**—with cold winters, warm summers, and plenty of variety in between.

- **Winter (December–February)**
  Winters in Pennsylvania can be **cold and snowy**, especially in the northern and western parts of the state. Temperatures often dip below freezing, and snow can cover the ground for days or weeks at a time. Cities like Erie and Scranton get more snow than places like Philadelphia.
  You'll need **boots, coats, gloves, and hats**, and you can expect chilly winds and icy mornings.

- **Spring (March–May)**
  Spring is when the world wakes back up. Flowers start

93

to **bloom**, trees turn green again, and animals come out of hiding. It's also a **muddy season**, with melting snow and plenty of spring showers.
Temperatures slowly climb from the 40s to the 70s (°F), and the air starts to smell fresh and full of life.

- **Summer (June–August)**
  Summers in Pennsylvania are **warm to hot**, especially in July and August. Temperatures can reach the **80s and 90s**, and it's usually humid, which means the air feels sticky. It's a great time for swimming, biking, and exploring lakes and forests.

- **Fall (September–November)**
  Fall brings **cooler air and changing leaves**. Temperatures drop back into the 50s and 60s, and the hills and mountains become a rainbow of **reds, oranges, and yellows**. It's a favorite season for many because of the beauty, the crisp weather, and cozy clothes like flannels and sweaters.

No matter what season you're in, Pennsylvania always has something interesting going on in the sky and all around you.

Seasonal Activities

Each season in Pennsylvania comes with **its own set of fun things to do**. The landscape and weather help create amazing outdoor adventures year-round.

- **Fall Leaf Peeping**
  "Leaf peeping" means traveling to see the **changing**

leaves, and Pennsylvania is one of the best places in the country for it. The **Pocono Mountains, Laurel Highlands**, and **State College** areas have especially beautiful displays. Many families take weekend drives just to admire the colors and take photos.

- **Winter Sledding and Snow Play**
  When snow falls, hills become sled runs! You'll also see kids building **snowmen**, having **snowball fights**, and maybe even **ice skating** or skiing in places like the Poconos.

- **Spring Hikes and Wildflowers**
  As things thaw out, trails reopen and **spring wildflowers** begin to bloom. You can spot **trillium, violets, and daffodils**, and listen to **frogs croaking and birds singing**.

- **Summer Lakes and Water Fun**
  Pennsylvania's many **lakes, rivers, and parks** make summer an ideal time for **boating, kayaking, fishing, and swimming**. Popular spots include **Lake Wallenpaupack, Presque Isle State Park**, and the **Delaware Water Gap**.

In every season, there's a way to get outside and **enjoy nature's show**.

Weather Patterns and Extremes

While Pennsylvania's weather is usually manageable, it can be **unpredictable** and occasionally **extreme**. Knowing what to expect helps keep people safe and prepared.

- **Thunderstorms**
  Common in **late spring and summer**, thunderstorms bring **heavy rain, lightning, thunder, and sometimes hail**. While most pass quickly, some can cause power outages or minor flooding.

- **Snowstorms**
  Large snowstorms, called **nor'easters**, can dump a foot or more of snow in a day. These storms can shut down schools, close roads, and create a winter wonderland—perfect for a day off and some snowy fun.

- **Occasional Tornadoes**
  Tornadoes are rare but not impossible in Pennsylvania. They mostly occur in **western and central parts** of the state and tend to be small compared to those in the Midwest. Still, weather alerts and safety drills help people stay safe.

- **Flooding and Fog**
  Rivers like the **Susquehanna and Delaware** can overflow after heavy rain or snowmelt. This can lead to **localized flooding**, especially in valleys and lowlands. In the morning, many areas—especially near rivers—may be covered in **thick fog**, making things look mysterious and quiet.

Pennsylvania weather keeps things interesting, and learning how it works can help you become a **mini meteorologist!**

How Nature Changes

As the seasons shift, so does **nature itself**. Animals, trees, flowers, and even insects adapt in amazing ways.

- **Fall Changes**
  Leaves change color as trees prepare for winter. Animals like **squirrels and chipmunks** collect food. **Bears** prepare to hibernate, and birds begin their **migration south**.

- **Winter Silence**
  Many animals **hibernate** or **stay hidden**, and the landscape becomes quiet. You might spot animal tracks in the snow, or see **deer and birds** searching for food.

- **Spring Awakenings**
  Birds return, frogs sing, and the air buzzes with new life. **Trees bud, flowers bloom**, and animals come out of hiding. Baby animals like **fawns, ducklings, and bunnies** are often spotted.

- **Summer Energy**
  Everything is full of life. **Fireflies flash**, **bees buzz**, and **animals roam** more freely. You might see **turtles basking in the sun**, or hear the hum of cicadas on warm nights.

By paying attention to these changes, you can **connect with the rhythm of the natural world**—and notice something new every season.

A State of Seasonal Wonders

Pennsylvania's ever-changing weather and four full seasons make it a place where **no two months feel the same**. From bundling up in winter snow to jumping in summer lakes, from watching fall leaves drift to spotting spring's first flower, each part of the year brings **fresh adventures and new discoveries**.

So whether you're out with your sled, on a hike in bloom-filled forests, or curled up watching a storm roll through, there's always something to appreciate about Pennsylvania's skies, seasons, and the world around you.

Chapter 17: Test Your Pennsylvania Knowledge!

You've explored Pennsylvania's history, nature, cities, food, sports, and science—now it's time to **see what you remember and have some fun** doing it! This chapter is packed with games, puzzles, trivia, and creative ideas to help you show off everything you've learned about the Keystone State.

Whether you're reading at home, riding in the car, or planning your next visit, these activities will help you feel like a true Pennsylvania pro!

Trivia Challenges

Ready for a quiz? Try these **fun and tricky questions** to test your Pennsylvania brainpower. Grab a pencil and circle your answers!

Multiple Choice:

1. What is Pennsylvania's nickname?

    o A. The Granite State

    o B. The Keystone State

    o C. The Garden State

    o D. The Show-Me State

2. What chocolate company was started in Pennsylvania?

- A. Nestlé

- B. Mars

- C. Hershey

- D. Cadbury

3. Which city is home to the Liberty Bell?

  - A. Pittsburgh

  - B. Erie

  - C. Harrisburg

  - D. Philadelphia

4. Who invented the polio vaccine in Pittsburgh?

  - A. Benjamin Franklin

  - B. Jonas Salk

  - C. Albert Einstein

  - D. Rachel Carson

5. Which famous amusement park has free admission?

  - A. Dutch Wonderland

  - B. Knoebels

o C. Dorney Park

   o D. Hersheypark

True or False:

6. The Pennsylvania Dutch are actually from the Netherlands.

7. Taylor Swift was born in Pennsylvania.

8. Eastern State Penitentiary is still an active prison today.

9. Scrapple is a kind of dessert made from apples.

10. The Liberty Bell has a crack in it.

Name That Place:

11. Which Pennsylvania town celebrates Groundhog Day every year?

12. What is the name of the natural canyon in north-central PA?

13. Which Pittsburgh museum is all about pop artist Andy Warhol?

14. What massive forest covers northwestern PA?

15. What historical building in Philadelphia is where the Declaration of Independence was signed?

(Answers appear at the end of the chapter!)

Map and Landmark Puzzles

Print or draw a blank **map of Pennsylvania**, and try to **label these places**:

- Philadelphia

- Pittsburgh

- Harrisburg (the capital!)

- Erie

- The Pocono Mountains

- Susquehanna River

- Pennsylvania Grand Canyon

- Hershey

- Valley Forge

- Gettysburg

Bonus challenge: Draw a small symbol to represent what each place is known for (chocolate, battlefields, mountains, rivers, etc.).

PA Bingo and Scavenger Hunt Ideas

Here's a fun **Pennsylvania BINGO** idea! Create a 5x5 grid and fill it with things like:

- Ate a Philly cheesesteak

- Visited a state park

- Saw a bald eagle

- Rode a train

- Toured an Amish market

- Tried birch beer

- Took a photo with the Liberty Bell

- Drove past a horse-drawn buggy

- Went to a museum

- Saw fall leaves change color

When you complete a row (horizontal, vertical, or diagonal), shout "PA BINGO!"

Or try a **road trip scavenger hunt**—see how many of these you can spot:

- A "Welcome to Pennsylvania" sign

- A covered bridge

- A Wawa or Sheetz store

- A silo or barn

- A deer or turkey

- A sign with a town name that makes you laugh (like Intercourse or Bird-in-Hand!)

- An Amish buggy

- A mural or street art

- A train or railroad crossing

- A Pennsylvania license plate with a cool design

These games make car rides or hometown explorations more exciting!

Sharing What You Learned

Now that you know so much about Pennsylvania, don't keep it to yourself—**spread the Keystone State pride!** Here are a few fun ideas:

- **Make a Pennsylvania scrapbook**
  Include photos, postcards, drawings, and facts from your favorite places.

- **Create a quiz for your family or friends**
  Use the trivia questions in this chapter—or invent your own—and see who knows the most!

- **Draw your own PA postcard**
  Design the front with a drawing of something iconic (like the Liberty Bell or a roller coaster), and on the back, write a fun fact.

- **Host a Pennsylvania-themed day**
  Eat pierogies or whoopie pies, play bingo, and watch a movie or show set in PA (*Rocky*, *National Treasure*, or *The Perks of Being a Wallflower* are a few that feature PA scenes—ask a grown-up first!).

- **Write a PA fact poem**
  Combine your knowledge into a fun poem:

  From Philly's bell to forest trails,
  From Hershey bars to Amish tales,
  In summer sun or winter snow,
  PA's the place you've got to go!

Quiz Answer Key

1. B — The Keystone State

2. C — Hershey

3. D — Philadelphia

4. B — Jonas Salk

5. B — Knoebels

6. False (They're German!)

7. True

8. False (It's a museum now)

9. False (It's a savory pork and cornmeal dish)

10. True

11. Punxsutawney

12. Pine Creek Gorge (Pennsylvania Grand Canyon)

13. Andy Warhol Museum

14. Allegheny National Forest

15. Independence Hall

Celebrate the Keystone State!

Pennsylvania is full of fascinating facts, awesome attractions, inspiring people, and beautiful places. Testing your knowledge and playing games makes learning even more fun—and now you can call yourself a true **Pennsylvania expert.**

Wherever you go in this amazing state, you'll be able to spot its treasures, understand its past, and appreciate its unique culture. So go ahead—share your new knowledge, plan your next adventure, and wear your **PA pride** with a big smile!

Made in United States
Troutdale, OR
04/22/2025

30827586R00060